P9-BYT-661

11118

Two-Hour Scrap Crafts

Anita Louise Crane

Two-Hour Scrap Crafts

Anita Louise Crane

Sterling Publishing Co., Inc. New York

A Sterling/Chapelle Book

Chapelle Limited

Owner: Jo Packham

Editor: Ann Bear

Staff: Areta Bingham, Kass Burchett, Marilyn Goff, Holly Hollingsworth, Will Jones, Susan Jorgensen, Barbara Milburn, Linda Orton, Karmen Quinney, Leslie Ridenour, Cindy Stoeckl, Gina Swapp, Sara Toliver

Photography: Kevin Dilley for Hazen Imaging, Inc.

Photo styling: Anita Louise Crane

Library of Congress Cataloging-in-Publication Data

Crane, Anita Louise.
  Two-hour scrap crafts / Anita Louise Crane.
    p. cm.
  "A Sterling/Chapelle book."
  ISBN 0-8069-8783-9
  1. Handicraft. 2. Scrap materials. I. Title

TT157.C713 2000
745.5--dc21   00-033900

10   9   8   7   6   5   4   3   2   1

Published by Sterling Publishing Company, Inc.
387 Park Avenue South, New York, N.Y. 10016
© 2000 by Anita Louise Crane
Distributed in Canada by Sterling Publishing
c/o Canadian Manda Group, One Atlantic Avenue, Suite 105
Toronto, Ontario, Canada M6K 3E7
Distributed in Great Britain and Europe by Cassell PLC
Wellington House, 125 Strand, London WC2R 0BB, England
Distributed in Australia by Capricorn Link (Australia) Pty Ltd.
P.O. Box 6651, Baulkham Hills, Business Centre, NSW 2153, Australia
Printed in the USA
All rights reserved

Sterling ISBN 0-8069-8783-9

We would like to offer our sincere appreciation of the valuable support given in this ever-changing industry of new ideas, concepts, designs and products developed by:

Pfaff American Sales Corp.
P.O. Box 566
Paramus, NJ 07653-0566
(201) 262-7211

Plaid Enterprises, Inc.
P.O. Box 117600
Norcross, GA 30091-7600
(770) 923-8200

Walnut Hollow
1409 State Road 23
Dodgeville, WI 53533
(800) 950-5101

If you have any questions or comments, please contact:
Chapelle Ltd.
P.O. Box 9252
Ogden, UT 84409

(801) 621-2777
Fax (801) 621-2788
chapelle@chapelleltd.com
www.chapelleltd.com

The written instructions, photographs, designs, and projects in this volume are intended for the personal use of the reader and may be reproduced for that purpose only. Any other use, especially commercial use, is forbidden under law without the written permission of the copyright holder.

Every effort has been made to ensure that all information in this book is accurate. However, due to differing conditions, tools, and individual skills, the publisher cannot be responsible for any injuries, losses, and/or other damages which may result from the use of the information in this book.

For my dear friend Missy in memory of her mother, Mary Lou Gilholm.

To Kathy Pace of Gooseberry Hill Notions, thank you for the beautiful antique lace and button lamp on page 57.

Thank you Carole Duh for the lovely doll on page 39 and for your Star Tree Topper pattern on page 111.

And to Sugar House Antique, thank you for the exquisite antique linens and laces that are used throughout this book.

A special thank you to Kathy Pace, Coalville, UT and Dixie Barber, Park City, UT for allowing us to photograph part of this book in their homes.

Anita Louise Crane has been designing, creating, photographing, painting, writing, and marketing since 1981. She is best known for her one-of-a-kind teddy bears.

She has been a special-occasion and wedding dress designer and seamstress, as well as proprietress of the Bearlace Cottage in Park City, Utah.

Anita currently runs her teddy bear business by appointment from her home. She specializes in her watercolor paintings and in the creation of teddy bears, bunnies, and mice. She has a wonderful collection of vintage laces and linens.

Anita is spending a significant amount of time these days in the creation of her craft project books, as well as illustrating and writing a children's book, which is the dream of her life.

She is the author of Teddy Bear Magic, Two-Hour Teddy Bears, Two-Hour Dolls' Clothes, Making Adorable Teddy Bears, and Adorable Furniture for Dolls and Teddy Bears.

Anita resides in Park City, Utah, with her husband Bruce and kitty, Raisen. She is the mother of four and grandmother of nine. She is usually busy stitching up slipcovers and creating decorative projects for her home. The remainder of her time is spent painting and enjoying the mountains.

Contents

The Best for a
Friend
5.0

For a Little
Friend
5.0

INTRODUCTION

We all have items in our house that we keep just in case we may need them some day. Sometimes we save even broken things, such as a favorite chipped plate from grandmother's cupboard. Some other common oddments include scraps from favorite fabrics that we refuse to throw away, jars and tins of buttons, lace remnants that are too lavish to toss, or pretty ribbons that we simply enjoy.

Now it is time to go through the attic, basement, and closet to see these discards in a new light. Those scraps of fabric, ribbons, trims, assorted buttons, and beads can be used to create lovely gifts and practical accessories. We have also included projects that will enhance the beauty of your home and save you dollars in the process.

Most of the projects in Two-Hour Scrap Crafts *can be mastered by a novice and will take less than two hours to complete. We have included projects that put to use broken china, recycled lamp shades, frames, and remnants. Step-by-step instructions provide a foundation to create designs of your very own. Beautiful photography of each project will inspire you with new ideas.*

A little glue, needle and thread, paint, and imagination make the possibilities endless. Have fun experimenting with new ideas and materials. Enjoy the process. Do not be concerned if you fall short of "perfection." You will learn something new with each step of the way and leave a small treasure, a remnant of yourself, behind. Happy creating!

Anita Louise Crane

Establish a Mood

*W*hether it is a well-set table, a romantic window treatment, or a simply perfect framed photograph, nothing puts family or friends at ease more than a comfortably decorated room.

The smallest details sometimes make all of the difference. The subtle placement of handmade boxes or linen napkins in shiny napkin rings help to establish a mood.

There is also a certain satisfaction that comes when the velvet-covered frame or the beautiful drapes were something that you created yourself from some of the scraps you have both collected and treasured.

*P*lace mats and napkins made from an old table-cloth can be part of a romantic table when placed with eclectic vintage china and silver.

INSTRUCTIONS:

1. Measure tablecloth to determine number of place mats that can be made.

Note: Standard size for place mats is 18" x 14" and napkins is 18" x 18". Adjust dimensions as desired.

2. Tear napkins and place mats from tablecloth.

Tip: Consider making a table runner from any leftover fabric.

3. Using needle and beginning at center of one side of place mat, remove one thread at a time from edge until fringe is desired size. Repeat for each edge.

4. Repeat Steps 2–3 for each remaining place mat and napkin.

Small pieces of old lace will help this tiny lamp shade brighten and beautify any shadowed space.

MATERIALS:

Tablecloth: loose-weave, toile or linen

EQUIPMENT:

Sewing needle
Tape measure

LACE-EDGED NAPKINS & TABLE SQUARE

*S*o very beautiful and even practical, these napkins can be easily made on an early Tuesday morning. The edges are pretty whether trimmed in lace or gently frayed. The same fabric for the napkins and table square create a mood that is both intimate and personal.

MATERIALS:

Fabric: loose-weave
Lace

EQUIPMENT:

Iron and ironing board
Sewing machine
Sewing needle

INSTRUCTIONS:

1. Cut fabric 13" square for napkins. Fold raw edges in ¼" and press. Fold in ¼" again and press.

2. Using sewing machine, stitch lace around edges of napkins.

3. Cut or tear fabric square for table square to desired dimensions.

4. Using needle and beginning at center of one side of table square, remove one thread at a time from edge until fringe is 1" long. Repeat for each edge.

There is a secret of a very select few who always make you feel at home, but who make certain nothing ever looks quite the same each time you are invited for lunch. They simply use what they have in different places and in different ways. Here table runners, scarves, and tablecloths have been layered gypsy style. Some are new, some are old, some are used for their intended purpose, and some not.

OVAL TABLE COVER

If you have a damaged table that your friends and family dislike, which you still love and use, dress it up with a lovely table cover. This table-top became warped after being left out in a rainstorm and the laminate top was peeled off. A table cover was a delightful way to not only "restore" the table, but add a spring-like cottage charm to my kitchen.

INSTRUCTIONS:

1. Place newspaper on flat surface. Place table upside down on newspaper. Trace around table and add ⅝" for pattern. Using craft scissors, cut out pattern.

2. Place and trace pattern onto fabric. Using fabric scissors, cut out fabric.

3. Measure circumference of table. Cut one strip from fabric 1½ times circumference x 12" for flounce.

Note: Strip may be made from two or more pieces if necessary.

4. Turn one long edge of flounce under 2" and press. Stitch in place.

5. Place short ends with right sides together and stitch.

6. Gather raw edge of flounce to fit circumference of table. Pin flounce to fabric top with right sides together and stitch edges.

MATERIALS:

Fabric or large tablecloth
Newspaper
Sewing thread

EQUIPMENT:

Fabric marker
Pencil
Scissors: craft; fabric
Sewing machine
Tape measure

Fabric scraps of faded chintz, gingham, soft paisley, or calico can easily be made into dresser scarves by tearing the fabric and fraying the edges. Change scarves with the season, one filled with birds for spring, plain white for summer, and acorns for fall.

FRAMED LACE

*L*ovely vintage lace scraps and antique, faded ribbons can be saved and shared in a much loved frame. One of the ribbon pieces in this frame was used as the background on my first business card and has sentimental meaning for me. The "picture of lace" paints a hundred memories that I instantly recall each time I sit having my afternoon tea.

MATERIALS:

Cardboard
Fabrics: silk, taffeta, or
  velvet
Felt
Foam-core board
Laces: assorted
Picture frame with
  glass
Ribbons: assorted
Sewing thread

EQUIPMENT:

Craft knife
Duct tape
Fabric marker
Fabric scissors
Iron and ironing board
Sewing needle
Straight pins
Tape measure

INSTRUCTIONS:

1. Using craft knife, cut foam-core board and cardboard to fit inside of picture frame.

2. Place foam-core board on felt. Trace around foam-core board and cut out.

3. Using craft glue, adhere felt onto one side of foam-core board.

4. Place foam-core board on wrong side of fabric. Trace around foam-core board. Add 2" to each side and cut out.

5. With felt side down, place and center foam-core board on fabric.

6. Fold fabric over sides to back of foam-core board and tape in place.

7. Fold fabric over top and bottom to back of foam-core board, squaring off corners. Tape in place.

8. Apply craft glue around edges of fabric. Place cardboard on top of fabric and adhere.

9. Press lace and ribbon pieces. Arrange lace and ribbon as desired. Pin in place.

10. Using needle and thread, tack lace and ribbon in place.

11. Optional: Place foam-core board in picture frame or have collage professionally framed.

FRAMED NEEDLEPOINT

An old needlepoint square that has been packed away will look lovely when placed in a vintage frame that was discovered in the attic or purchased at a Saturday morning yard sale. If your frame is too large, set the needlepoint on a piece of faded fabric or scraps of London lace.

INSTRUCTIONS:

1. Using craft knife, cut foam-core board and cardboard to fit inside of frame.

2. Using fabric scissors, cut fabric 2" larger than foam-core board.

3. Using needle and thread, tack edges of needlepoint to fabric. If frame is larger than needlepoint, fold edges of needlepoint under and tack onto center of fabric.

4. Place fabric right side down on work surface. Center and place foam-core board on fabric. Pull fabric over sides of foam-core board and tape in place. Fold corners neatly and pull fabric over top and bottom of foam-core board. Tape in place.

5. Place needlepoint into frame. Place cardboard into back of frame until flush with frame edge.

6. Cut kraft paper same size as outside dimensions of frame. Adhere kraft paper onto back of frame.

7. Attach picture frame hanger onto frame.

MATERIALS:

Cardboard
Fabric
Foam-core board
Kraft paper
Needlepoint
Picture frame
Picture frame hanger

EQUIPMENT:

Craft knife
Duct tape
Fabric scissors
Spray adhesive

"Scrap" as defined in Websters is "fragment, section, segment, sample..." which means that tiny flowers, collected on a summer's day may also be considered scraps. Press to dry each one, then gently place on a piece of handmade paper for framing.

VELVET EMBELLISHED FRAMES

*C*ustom-made frames can be expensive and so very perfect, while those made by hand are created with small, loving imperfections and dressed up in fabrics from old prom dresses and lace saved from someone's wedding veil. These are the frames that will be saved and given from mother to daughter to granddaughter.

VELVET AND LACE

MATERIALS:

Cardboard
Fabric glue
Laces: assorted widths
Photograph or art
Picture mat
Velvet

EQUIPMENT:

Craft knife
Fabric scissors
Hot-glue gun and glue
   sticks

INSTRUCTIONS:

1. Using craft knife, cut cardboard to same outside dimensions as mat.

2. Place mat with right side down on wrong side of velvet. Using fabric scissors, cut velvet 1" wider on all sides than mat.

3. Trim corners on the diagonal as shown in Illustration 1.

4. Using scissors, cut velvet inside mat in an "X".

5. Fold inside velvet edges to back side of mat, trimming as necessary. Using hot-glue gun, adhere velvet onto mat.

6. Fold outside velvet edges to back side of mat and adhere.

7. Using fabric glue, adhere lace onto front of mat as desired. Fold lace ends to back side of mat as shown in Illustration 2.

8. Place and arrange photograph or art behind mat opening.

9. Using hot-glue gun, adhere cardboard onto back of photograph and frame.

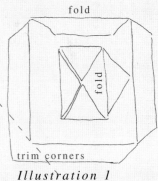

Illustration 1

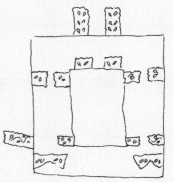

Illustration 2

VELVET AND RIBBON

MATERIALS:

Cardboard

Craft glue

Fabric

Glass (cut to desired
  size)

Picture frame hanger

Pressed flowers and
  ferns

Ribbon: 1"-wide satin;
  ¾"–1"-wide velvet

Sewing thread

EQUIPMENT:

Craft Knife

Fabric scissors

Hot-glue gun and glue
  sticks

Sewing needle

INSTRUCTIONS:

1. Using craft knife, cut cardboard to same dimensions as glass.

2. Using fabric scissors, cut fabric to same dimensions as glass.

3. Using craft glue, adhere fabric onto cardboard.

4. Adhere flowers and ferns onto fabric.

5. Place glass on pressed arrangement and using hot-glue gun, adhere edges of glass onto edges of cardboard.

6. Cut velvet ribbon to dimensions of frame, mitering corners.

7. Adhere velvet ribbon to outside edges of glass as shown in Illustration 1.

8. Make bow by folding and tacking satin ribbon as shown in Illustration 2.

9. Attach picture frame hanger onto frame.

Illustration 1

Illustration 2

STILL-LIFE ART PILLOWS

A *favorite piece of art that your sister saved, a photograph that makes you smile, a card sent from a special friend — each can be color-copied on heat transfer paper and then made into a pillow for your favorite chair in your own personal hideaway.*

INSTRUCTIONS:

1. Determine pillow size based on sizes of art and scraps.

2. Using iron, transfer art onto muslin, following manufacturer's instructions.

3. Trim artwork, leaving ½" border all around.

4. Cut two pieces from fabric the same width as art and length as desired.

5. Cut two pieces from fabric the same length as art and width as desired.

6. Using sewing machine, stitch fabric to top and bottom of art with right sides together.

7. Stitch lace along top and bottom of art.

8. Stitch fabric to side of art and fabric with right sides together. Repeat with remaining piece.

9. Stitch lace along sides of art and fabric.

10. Cut one piece each from batting and fabric to same dimensions as top for back.

11. Place back of pillow front on batting and pin in place.

12. Embellish with ribbons and lace trim as desired. Using needle and thread, quilt around details for dimension.

Note: Stitch as little or as much as desired.

13. Using sewing machine, stitch pillow front and back pieces with right sides together, leaving 3" opening. Trim corners and turn pillow cover right side out.

14. Stuff pillow with polyester stuffing. Using needle and thread, stitch opening closed.

15. Optional: Pin cording around outside edge of pillow and hand-stitch in place.

Whimsy has its basis in creativity, so do not forget to shape your pillow or make photo on page 35 an overall pattern.

MATERIALS:

Braided cording
  (optional)
Fabrics: muslin; printed
Heat-transfer art
Lace trim
Polyester stuffing
Quilt batting: low-loft

EQUIPMENT:

Iron and ironing board
Sewing machine
Sewing needle
Straight pins
Tape measure

The cording on the pillow above was covered with matching fabric and sandwiched between the pillow front and back before stitching them together.

- Cut the fabric 1½ times the length of the cording x 3" wide.

- Fold fabric around cording with wrong sides together and baste raw edges ¼" from cording.

- Gather fabric evenly to same length as cording.

LACE WINDOW DRAPES

When I see fabric that I really love, I always buy five or six yards. If I love it, I know it will look perfect in any corner of my home. These window coverings were inspired by one of my favorite fabrics. It reminded me of spring, so I added a lace valance, a linen tablecloth, and embroidered sheets.

MATERIALS:

Adhesive hem tape
Floral fabric
Heavy-duty thread
Lace: 14"-wide with
   scalloped edge
Lace tablecloth: large
   enough to fit window
Nails: copper or gold
Ribbon (optional)
Wooden curtain rings
Wooden curtain rod and
   brackets

EQUIPMENT:

Hammer
Sewing machine
Sewing needle
Straight pins

INSTRUCTIONS:

1. Using hammer, place nails above window. Hang lace tablecloth by slipping lace edges over nail heads.

Note: Spacing between nails is determined by the desired finished look. Space nails close together for a gathered look and far apart for flat look.

2. Attach curtain rod and brackets above window.

3. Measure length required for panel curtains. Cut two panels from floral fabric.

Note: Standard 84" panels require 2½ yards of fabric per panel. To puddle curtains add one yard to length.

4. Hem both ends of floral panels with adhesive hem tape, following manufacturer's instructions.

5. Attach wooden rings to top of panels and hang on rods.

6. Hang or pin 14" lace over top of curtains for valance.

7. Optional: Tie curtains back with ribbon.

Do you see an old dishtowel, a little bit of lace, and the edge of your grandmother's crocheted doily, or an enchanting cover to a door?

Vintage tambour lace used for custom-fitted curtains, linen table napkins draped as valances over rods, and a sage fabric draped and tied with tassels from my collection give an elegant styling to French doors in this lovely guest room.

TAILORED CHAIR COVER

When wildflowers are in bloom, it is time to stitch up a Spring wardrobe for your home. What are chairs wearing this spring? Fashion forecasts call for a bit of flounce, faded fabrics, scalloped skirts, lace trims, and corded edgings. Enjoy them as you sip your morning coffee or afternoon tea.

INSTRUCTIONS:

1. Take chair measurements as shown in Illustration 1.

2. Cut two pieces of fabric to fit chair back, allowing for ½" seam allowances. Cut lace the width of chair back, allowing for ½" seam allowance.

3. Pin lace to front piece of chair back.

4. Measure sides and top of chair back. Cut cording to this length plus 1". Cut fabric strip to this length plus 1" x 2" wide.

5. Place fabric strip right side down on work surface. Place cording lengthwise along center of strip and fold fabric over. Using zipper foot, stitch along cording to make welting as shown in Illustration 2.

6. Sandwich welting between chair back pieces with cording side in and right sides together. Stitch sides and top of chair back pieces as shown in Illustration 3. Turn right side out.

7. Place over chair back and make any necessary adjustments.

MATERIALS:

Cording: cotton
Fabric
Lace
Sewing thread

EQUIPMENT:

Fabric marker
Fabric scissors
Iron and ironing board
Sewing machine and
   zipper foot
Straight pins
Tape measure

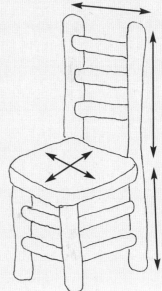

Illustration 1

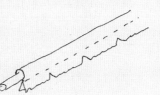

Illustration 2

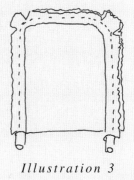

Illustration 3

8. Cut one piece of fabric to fit chair seat, allowing for ½" seam allowance.

9. Pin chair seat to front of chair back with right sides together. Place on chair and make any necessary adjustments.

10. Measure circumference of chair seat. Drop length is the distance from top of chair seat to ground. Cut fabric to circumference plus 17" x drop length plus 2".

11. Fold hem under 1½" and press. Stitch hem in place. Fold sides in ½" and press. Stitch sides in place.

12. Pin skirt to front and sides of chair seat and to chair back with right sides together. Adjust fabric for corner gathers. Allow 4" of fabric for each corner pleat.

13. Place on chair with open side of skirt in back. Make any necessary adjustments.

To make a fitted skirt with a scalloped edge, cut fabric to desired length and cut scallops on bottom edge as desired.

- Cut lining to match fabric scallop. With right sides together, stitch skirt to lining. Trim seams, cut curves, and turn right side out. Press.

- With right sides together, pin raw edge of skirt to seat, easing around corners. Stitch together.

I am always buying remnants of three or four yards, not knowing what I will use them for. Perhaps a snowy day will inspire me to slip-cover the armchair that my cat has been sharpening his claws on. I will have to use several different fabrics, as I rarely have exactly enough. I usually pick fabrics in the same color range because I like them and so I know they will go together. These whimsical slipcovers are fun, and look much better than what is under them. Or perhaps you have a very "nice" chair you simply want to protect.

- Be certain to wash fabrics first.

- To add a skirt, use a scrap of old crochet.

- To cover a seam, drape a pretty lace-edged tea towel.

- Assorted throw pillows add the finishing touch.

- Fabric for back of chair and under seat cushion may be a muslin scrap.

It is not surprising at all that when you look into the pictures of this book you imagine a washed blue country cottage mellowed with age and tucked serenely at the foot of the rocky mountains.

The sense of this place is one of old-fashioned country comforts as well as one of belonging. Its kitchen with its village fare is at this home's heart. For this is where when friends come to call, refreshments are served and the front door is left half open so the smell of fresh country air and wild roses fill the room.

DISHWASHER COVER

Sometimes the new and practical simply does not belong with the ruffled and romantic. In a case such as this, simply cover it up! Here a charming ruffled cover can be easily removed whenever the dishes need to be done.

INSTRUCTIONS:

1. Measure dimensions of dishwasher below control panel and add ¾" to height and 1½" to width. Cut one piece to these dimensions from batting and each fabric, for front and back.

2. Sandwich batting between fabrics with right sides out and pin layers together. Using sewing needle and thread, baste together.

3. Using sewing machine, quilt rows 1½" apart from top to bottom.

4. Cut or tear two 2" strips from contrasting (back) fabric for side bindings and one for top binding. Cut or tear one 3" strip for bottom edge.

5. Place 2" strips on back of cover and stitch in place. Fold strips to front of cover.

6. Turn raw edges under and stitch to front of cover.

7. Repeat Steps 5 and 6 for top strip.

8. Fold one long edge of bottom strip under ½" and press. Stitch in place.

9. Place unfinished edge of bottom strip on front of cover with right sides together. Stitch in place. Fold side edges over to back of cover and stitch in place.

10. Measure control panel. Cut one strip 1½ times the width of the control panel x length plus ⅝" from fabric for ruffle. Cut one strip 1½ times the width x 2⅝" length from contrasting fabric.

11. Turn sides of ruffle under ½" and press. Stitch in place.

MATERIALS:

Fabrics: contrasting (2)
Quilt batting: low-loft
Sewing thread
Velcro® strips: self-
    adhesive

EQUIPMENT:

Fabric scissors
Iron and ironing board
Sewing machine
Sewing needle
Straight pins
Tape measure

12. Turn bottom of ruffle under 1" and press. Stitch in place.

13. Turn edges of contrasting strip in ½" and press.

14. Pin contrasting strip to ruffle 1" above hem on right side and topstitch.

15. Gather-stitch top of ruffle with two rows of stitches. Gather ruffle and adjust to fit width of control panel.

16. Cut one strip from fabric the width of control panel plus 1" x 3". Fold strip with right sides together in half lengthwise and stitch ends to make band for ruffle.

17. Turn right side out. Pin one long edge of band to front side of ruffle. Stitch in place.

18. Pull band up and over gathered edge. Fold raw edge under and stitch in place.

19. Stitch Velcro strips to top edge of ruffle and around edges of quilted cover.

20. Remove tape from opposite side of strips and adhere onto dishwasher. Place ruffle and cover on dishwasher.

A special touch and a delight to use when guest offer to help with dinner dishes are these fabric-lined dish towels. You will need fabric, a hand towel, sewing thread, fabric scissors, and a sewing machine.

- Cut fabric to same dimensions as towel.

- Using sewing machine, stitch fabric to towel with right sides together, leaving one short end open. Turn right side out.

- Turn remaining edges under and stitch closed.

An eclectic use of cotton fabrics and antique cross-stitched napkins adorn and cover open spaces in this hutch.

➧ Using sewing machine, stitch 1" rod pockets on each end and hang as curtains.

TOASTER COVER

*T*hreads and patterns, fabrics and needles — these are the things of quiet afternoons. Make a sundress for a summer party or a cover-up for something used every day.

MATERIALS:

Bias tape
Fabrics (2)
Sewing thread

EQUIPMENT:

Fabric scissors
Quilt batting: low-loft
Sewing machine
Sewing needle
Straight pins
Tape measure

INSTRUCTIONS:

1. Measure toaster as shown in Illustration 1.

2. Cut one rectangle from first fabric to dimensions and add 1" to short side for Measurement 1. Cut two rectangles to dimensions and add 1" to sides and add ½" to top for Measurement 2. Repeat with second fabric for lining.

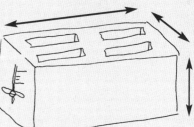

Illustration 1

3. Fold all pieces in half lengthwise and mark centers with line.

4. Match center lines on first fabric side pieces to center pieces with right sides together. Using sewing machine, stitch pieces together as shown in Illustration 2. Repeat with second fabric.

5. Place first fabric piece on batting and cut out batting.

6. Sandwich and pin batting between first and second fabric pieces with right sides out. Using sewing needle and thread, baste together.

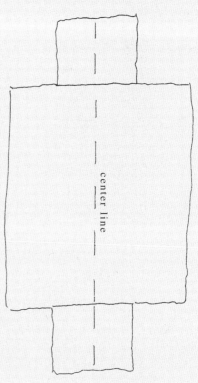

Illustration 2

7. Using sewing machine, stitch several straight rows horizontally. Stitch several rows vertically.

8. Stitch corners with right sides of first fabric together as shown in Illustration 3.

9. Stitch bias tape around bottom edge of cover.

Note: Always keep toaster unplugged when covered.

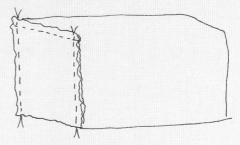

Illustration 3

SILK ROSE STATIONERY BOX

As a young girl, I filled empty boxes with pieces of paper that I would cut to letter size and paint with my initials or a picture of my kitty. I guess I was always fascinated with not only the writing of notes to my friends, but with the paper they were written on and the boxes in which I stored them.

MATERIALS:

Box with lid
Braid
Decoupage medium
Fabric
Lace
Silk rose

EQUIPMENT:

Fabric scissors
Hot-glue gun and glue
  sticks
Paintbrush: 1" flat

INSTRUCTIONS:

1. Cut fabric to lid dimensions.

2. Decoupage fabric onto top of box, following manufacturer's instructions.

3. Using hot-glue gun, adhere lace around edge of lid.

4. Adhere braid onto lace.

5. Cut two pieces of braid long enough to wrap around box and tie into bows.

6. Place one piece of braid at each end of box and tie bow for closure. Tie rose into one bow on lid.

7. Optional: If box bottom is not completely covered when lid is on, decoupage fabric onto box bottom.

On a quiet street, in a tiny mountain town, it is not unusual for friends to gather, to trade collected treasures, and share an afternoon with strawberry lemonade.

TAPESTRY BAGS

S impler summer days — a long walk to the local market, an afternoon in the meadow picking wildflowers, an evening spent with friends knitting sweaters for the winter frost ahead. The objects for each of these activities can be neatly packed into my handmade bag.

SHOULDER BAG

MATERIALS:

Fabrics: cotton; tapestry
Sewing thread

EQUIPMENT:

Scissors: craft; fabric
Sewing machine
Straight pins
Tape measure

INSTRUCTIONS:

1. Enlarge Shoulder Bag Pattern 285% on page 48 and photocopy. Using craft scissors, cut out pattern.

2. Fold fabric as shown in Illustration 1. Place top and side of pattern on fold. Pin fabric onto tapestry and cut out two pieces for shell. Repeat with cotton for lining.

3. Stitch sides of shell with right sides together. Stitch across bottom of shell. Trim excess fabric. Zigzag-stitch raw edges. Repeat for lining.

4. Fold corners of shell and stitch to make paper bag corners as shown in Illustration 2. Repeat for lining. Trim excess fabric.

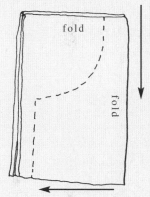

Illustration 1

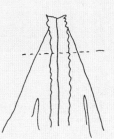

Illustration 2

5. Insert lining into shell, aligning seams. Pin in place. Stitch around one side of handle to top of bag as shown in Illustration 3.

6. Turn bag right side out. Fold raw edges in and topstitch opening closed. Topstitch opposite side of bag opening.

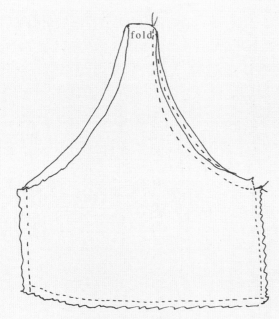

Illustration 3

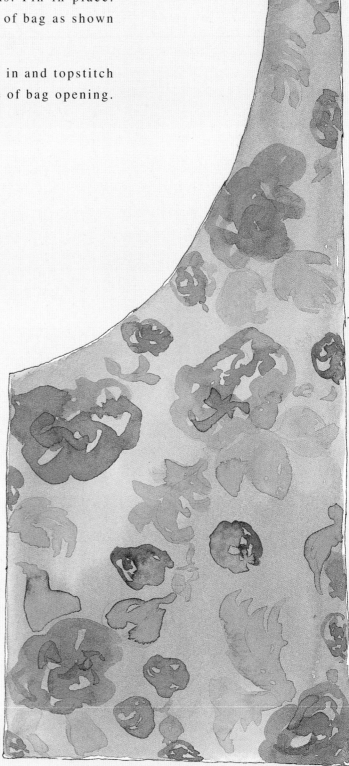

place on fold

place on fold

Shoulder Bag Pattern (enlarge 285%)

Right: Tiny pockets for lucky coins, needle and thread, or jewelry that needs to be hidden are a gift any hostess will love or can simply be the perfect addition to your tapestry bag.

FLAP BAG

MATERIALS:

Button: decorative,
    large
Fabrics: cotton; tapestry
Sewing thread

EQUIPMENT:

Fabric scissors
Sewing machine
Sewing needle
Straight pins
Tape measure
Velcro® closure

INSTRUCTIONS:

1. Determine finished size of bag. Cut rectangle from tapestry for shell, allowing ⅝" all around for seam allowances. Repeat with cotton for lining.

2. Place lining and shell with right sides together. Trim one end in a "V" or "U" for flap.

3. Using sewing machine, stitch around lining and shell, leaving bottom edge unstitched. Trim seams. Turn right side out.

4. Fold raw edges in and stitch closed.

5. Fold up bottom with shell sides together, leaving flap free. Stitch sides. Turn right side out.

6. Using needle and thread, attach button to outside of flap. Attach Velcro closure to inside of flap.

There are several different ways in which lace can be attached to shelves:

- A staple gun is a more permanent way to attach lace and works best on kitchen cupboards.

- Tiny copper-head nails work well on shelves. Lace can be hung over nails as shown in Illustration 1.

Tip: Space nails approximately 6" apart.

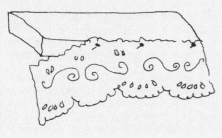

Illustration 1

- Velcro is self-adhesive or can be stitched onto fabric and stapled onto cupboards or shelves.

- Attractively drape laces on china cabinet shelves and allow dishes to hold them in place.

All of the above methods of attachment allow for lace to be removed and laundered, although some are easier to remove than others. Be certain that you take this into consideration before attaching lace.

Lace trim on a shelf's edge can add a romantic feminine touch to a family kitchen or other rooms where ladies come to call. It softens, it is enchanting, and it is so completely what a lady loves.

Grandma's tea cups, boxes filled with old love letters, an elaborate collection of vintage teapots — each is made even more special with crocheted doilies, pieces of old lace, or edgings removed from garments long ago discarded.

FABRIC & RIBBON MEMORY BOARD

An old mirror frame found at a country flea market could be covered with fabric and embellished with ribbons to make a beautiful as well as functional memory board. I had an antique frame sitting around that I wanted to use — and what better use than to show off dear family photographs and letters I read over and over again.

INSTRUCTIONS:

1. Using craft knife, cut foam-core board to fit inside of frame.

2. Using fabric scissors, cut fabric 3" larger all around than foam-core board.

3. Place and center foam-core board on wrong side of fabric. Pull fabric over sides to back of foam-core board and tape in place.

4. Keeping corners neat, pull fabric over top and bottom to back of foam-core board. Tape in place.

5. Criss-cross ribbon and tape to back of foam-core board.

6. Place foam-core board into frame. Tape postal paper over back of frame for cover.

7. Attach hanger to back of frame.

8. Attach silk flower and lace on board as desired.

MATERIALS:

Fabric
Foam-core board: ⅜" thick
Lace
Picture frame
Picture frame hanger
Postal paper
Ribbon
Silk flower

EQUIPMENT:

Craft knife
Duct tape
Fabric scissors

FABRIC & SHELL TRAY

*T*his lovely tray enhanced by a linen scrap and collected shells lends a personal place for handmade stationery, old ink pens, and other treasures that inspire beautifully handwritten words.

MATERIALS:

Cardboard (optional)
Fabric: linen or
    jacquard
Shells: assorted
Wicker tray

EQUIPMENT:

Craft knife
Fabric scissors
Hot-glue gun and glue
    sticks
Iron and ironing board
Tape measure

INSTRUCTIONS:

1. Measure inside dimensions of tray and add 1" to all sides. Using fabric scissors, cut out fabric to these dimensions. Optional: Using craft knife, cut out cardboard to fit inside dimensions of tray.

2. Cover cardboard with fabric and hot-glue excess onto back of cardboard. Insert cardboard into tray.

Note: This step applies if the bottom of the wicker tray does not have a smooth wooden lining.

3. Fit fabric to inside of tray and fold excess fabric under. Remove fabric and press.

4. Hot-glue fabric onto inside of tray.

5. Arrange shells as desired in tray. Hot-glue shells in place.

A lace-covered tray on a table layered in lace makes a very pleasant setting for fresh flowers and a favorite piece of art.

TO LIGHT THE WAY

On a cold winter evening when the wind blows the snow in mounds beneath the windows is the time to curl up with your favorite reading lamp, a good book, and a purring cat. These are the quiet pleasures for which we yearn, no matter what fills each of our days.

Creating something truly beautiful with scraps and remnants can be as simple as pinning a beautiful, but little used, lace collar or lace remnant around the top of a white lamp shade. Wrap a pretty ribbon scrap, then pin it with a silk flower arrangement at the top; or use a combination of lace pieces and a button-filled base.

MOSAIC LAMP BASE

*B*its and pieces of broken china — mother's favorite coffee cup, the handle from great-grandma's gravy bowl, Hanna's baby mug — combined with a cherished watercolor card or a beloved photograph are the scraps necessary for the base of this treasured lamp.

MATERIALS:

Acrylic paint: lt. gold
Ceramic glue
China plates
Decoupage medium
Gesso
Greeting card art
Premixed grout
Wooden lamp base:
  square

EQUIPMENT:

Clean rag
Duct tape
Hammer
Old towel
Paintbrush: 1" flat
Putty knife
Safety glasses
Sponge
Tile nippers

INSTRUCTIONS:

1. Paint lamp base with gesso. Allow to dry.

2. Paint lamp base with lt. gold. Allow to dry.

3. Decoupage art onto one panel of lamp base, following manufacturer's instructions.

4. Cover back of china plates with duct tape.

5. Wrap china plate in towel. Wearing safety glasses and using hammer, strike back side of china plate lightly to break into small pieces.

6. Unwrap china plate, leaving duct tape on back so pattern stays together. Repeat for each plate.

7. With a daub of glue, adhere china shards onto lamp base as desired, leaving about ¼" space between pieces.

Note: Use nippers to trim off sharp edges and to fit. Allow to dry.

8. Mix small amount of paint into grout.

Note: Too much paint will dilute grout and make it difficult to work with.

9. Using putty knife, apply grout over china shards, filling in spaces between shards. Using damp sponge, wipe excess grout from china shards.

RIBBON LAMP SHADE

Even in a country cottage, one often wishes for a touch of imperial grace. Royalty from ages past adorned their favorite belongings in the richest of velvets. A tiny touch of such finery recalls a decidedly more elegant time.

MATERIALS:

Premade lamp shade
Velvet cord trim
Velvet ribbon

EQUIPMENT:

Fabric glue

INSTRUCTIONS:

1. Adhere one end of ribbon to top of lamp shade. Begin wrapping ribbon vertically around lamp shade until covered. Tuck end under and adhere in place.

2. Adhere trim around top of lamp shade.

3. Tie bow with ribbon and adhere to top of lamp shade.

Adding small beads, whether new or vintage, lends a very special touch.

FITTED LAMP SHADE

Imagine some of the shaping and details of couture dressmaking applied to the shade of your lamp. It would be feminine, all about softness, and remind us to slow down, dress thoughtfully, and take time to feel like a lady.

INSTRUCTIONS:

1. Pin muslin to one section of lamp shade as shown in Illustration 1.

2. Using fabric marker, trace section shape, following wire ribs, onto muslin as shown in Illustration 2. Add ⅝" to each side and 1" to top and bottom of panel. Cut out muslin for panel pattern.

3. Pin muslin to fabric and cut out required number of panels for lamp shade.

4. Using sewing machine and with right sides together, stitch panel sides together with ⅝" seam allowances.

5. Pull stitched fabric over lamp shade with wrong side out and line up seams with wire ribs. Using straight pins, adjust seams as shown in Illustration 3 until fabric fits snugly.

6. Remove fabric from lamp shade and stitch any necessary adjustments. Trim excess fabric ¼" from seams.

(Continued on page 64)

MATERIALS:

Fabrics: cotton; muslin
Fabric glue
Fabric lamp shade
Sewing thread

EQUIPMENT:

Fabric marker
Fabric scissors
Safety pins
Sewing machine
Sewing needle
Straight pins
Tape measure

Illustration 1   *Illustration 2*    *Illustration 3*

(Continued from page 62)

7. Turn fabric right side out and place over lamp shade. Turn on lamp and adjust fabric, making certain that stitched seams line up with wire ribs. Pin fabric in place with safety pins.

Note: The light from the lamp will help insure seams are lined up properly.

8. Trim excess fabric from top and bottom, leaving ½" for turning under. Turn top edge under. Using sewing needle and thread, overlap-stitch hem in place.

9. Measure bottom circumference of lamp shade. Cut a strip 1½ times circumference x 2½" wide for ruffle.

10. Fold one long edge under ¼" and press. Fold ¼" again and press. Stitch in place.

11. Stitch narrow ends of ruffle with right sides together.

12. Gather-stitch raw edge of ruffle. Gather ruffle to fit bottom edge of lamp shade.

13. Place gathered edge of ruffle under bottom edge of lamp shade. Using needle and thread, tack ruffle in place. Steam seam down with iron.

14. Measure top circumference of lamp shade. Cut one piece each on bias from fabric, using circumference measurements x 2".

15. Fold in and press each long side of bias strip ⅝".

16. Adhere bias strip around top of shade.

A scrap of lace and lace trim is just what this simple lamp shade needs. Crystal drops may be added to the bottom edge of a lace covered lamp shade to add a certain charm and elegance.

The Best For A Guest

*W*hat could be more wonderful than creating thoughtful accessories for company to make them feel like royalty? Welcome them with comfortable, yet sophisticated things that say "you deserve the best."

Such touches create places to dream. Make magical window seats, perfect for spending your happiest afternoons; or turn lovely sitting rooms into private personal retreats.

NEEDLE-POINT PILLOW

how off that favorite needlepoint piece by making it into a pillow. This completed, but never used needlepoint piece was purchased at an antique sale several years ago. When I bought it, I knew that it would make a lovely pillow or chair seat. After several months of choosing between tassels, trims, and laces, I decided to frame my newly acquired treasure simply with a pleated ruffle.

MATERIALS:

Fabric
Needlepoint art
Polyester stuffing or
    pillow form
Sewing thread

EQUIPMENT:

Fabric scissors
Iron and ironing board
Sewing machine
Sewing needle
Straight pins
Tape measure

INSTRUCTIONS:

1. Cut two strips from fabric the same length as sides of needlepoint art and width as desired.

2. Using sewing machine, stitch fabric strips with right sides together to sides of needlepoint art for pillow front as shown in Illustration 1.

Illustration 1

3. Cut one strip each from fabric the same lengths as top and bottom of pillow front.

4. Stitch fabric strips with right sides together to top and bottom of pillow front as shown in Illustration 2.

Illustration 2

5. Lay pillow front right side down on fabric and cut out pillow back.

6. Cut or tear one strip 3" x 2 times the circumference of pillow for ruffle.

7. Fold strip in half lengthwise and press. Using sewing machine, stitch pleats as shown in Illustration 3.

8. Pin ruffle to pillow front as shown in Illustration 4.

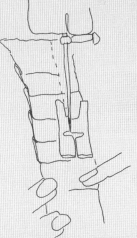

Illustration 3

Illustration 4

9. Stitch pillow front to back with right sides together, leaving an opening large enough to stuff with polyester stuffing or insert pillow form. Trim corners and turn right side out.

10. Stuff or place pillow form into cover. Using needle, and thread, stitch opening closed.

This lovely pillow sham was made from a lace tablecloth.

- Measure pillow and add ⅝" to two sides for seam allowance.

- Fold tablecloth in half and cut out sham with folded side on bottom and scalloped edges at top.

- Stitch sides of sham with right sides together.

LACE PILLOWS

hese scrap-lace pillows can be made in assorted sizes and shapes, and are easy to create. Allow lace scraps to dictate the sizes and shapes of the pillows. Lay lace scraps over different types of fabric to see which effect you like best. I like to make up several at a time so I have a special handmade gift for last minute gift-giving.

MATERIALS:

Fabrics: floral; lace
Lace
Polyester stuffing
Ribbons: assorted
 (optional)
Sewing thread

EQUIPMENT:

Fabric marker
Pencil
Scissors: craft; fabric
Sewing machine
Sewing needle
Straight pins
Tracing paper

INSTRUCTIONS:

1. Using tracing paper and pencil, trace Heart Pattern on page 96. Using craft scissors, cut out pattern.

Note: Heart Pattern may be enlarged or reduced as desired.

2. Trace pattern onto doubled floral fabric. Using fabric scissors, cut out two pieces.

3. Place and pin lace scraps over one side of fabric in a collage.

Tip: Place finished edges of lace over raw edges.

4. Optional: Ribbons may be added to lace collage.

5. Using needle and thread, tack lace and ribbons down with tiny stitches. Trim edges, if necessary.

6. Place front and back pillow pieces with right sides together. Using sewing machine, stitch sides together with ½" seam allowance, leaving 1" opening. Trim corners and clip curves.

7. Turn pillow right side out and stuff with polyester stuffing.

8. Using needle and thread, stitch opening closed.

Pieces whose simplicity makes them much sought after can be created in minutes from pieces of older fabrics that have been hand-painted.

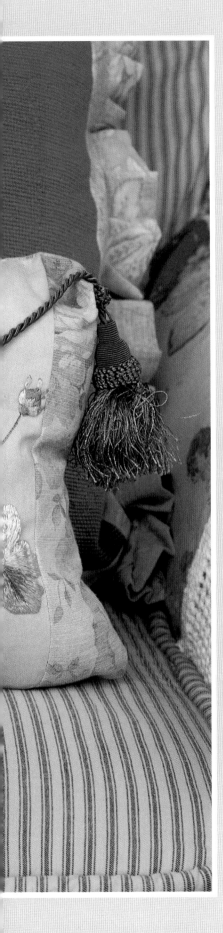

*M*ake a pillow from a vintage embroidered piece of fabric. The fabric I selected from my collection was too small for the pillow form. I was pleased, however, because I could add a favorite piece of faded fabric to the ends and back. For the finishing touch, I added a tasseled tieback.

MATERIALS:

Fabric: antique, coordi-
   nating pattern
Pillow form
Sewing thread
Tasseled tieback

EQUIPMENT:

Fabric scissors
Sewing machine
Sewing needle
Tape measure

INSTRUCTIONS:

1. Measure pillow form and add ⅝" all around for seam allowance. Using these measurements, cut out pillow front and pillow back from fabrics.

Note: Two strips of coordinating fabric may be cut and stitched to antique fabric, allowing ⅝" for seam allowances.

2. Using sewing machine, stitch front onto back with right sides together, leaving opening large enough to insert pillow form. Trim corners and turn right side out.

3. Place pillow form into cover. Using needle, and thread, stitch opening closed.

4. Stitch one tassel to each upper corner, allowing cording to drape down pillow.

Make pretty tea towels inexpensively by adding a narrow or wide band of fabric. Each of the lovely new pieces will add a breath of spring to your kitchen or make a lovely gift for your guest.

MATERIALS:

Fabric
Tea towel

EQUIPMENT:

Fabric scissors
Iron and ironing board
Sewing machine
Tape measure

INSTRUCTIONS:

1. Measure width of towel and add 1". Cut strip from fabric 3" x width of towel.

2. Fold all edges of fabric under ½" and press.

3. Place fabric on towel and stitch in place.

Above: Stitch remnant lengths of lace onto pillowcase edges to create a richly romantic look. These make an elegant gift when tied with an organdy bow and red rose.

Left: Guest towels are the most traditional way to decorate for guests. These are taken out when a guest will spend the night, or use them to make the family feel special.

- Using sewing machine, zigzag-stitch lace to bottom edge of towel.

- Optional: Stitch lace medallion to towel.

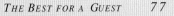

MATELASSÉ BEDSPREAD CURTAINS

hese curtains are made from recycled Matelassé twin-sized bedspreads. Because all edges are hemmed, they did not require any additional finishing, other than attaching tabs for hanging and lace scrap tiebacks. A lace tablecloth underpanel allows the morning sun to filter through.

MATERIALS:

Bedspreads: twin size, Matelassé or jacquard (2)
Dowel curtain rod and brackets
Fabric
Lace
Sewing thread

EQUIPMENT:

Fabric scissors
Iron and ironing board
Sewing machine
Straight pins

INSTRUCTIONS:

1. Cut fourteen strips from fabric 4"-wide x long enough to slide over curtain rod when finished for tabs.

2. Fold long raw edges under ½" and press.

3. Zigzag-stitch edges in place.

4. Evenly space and pin tabs to top of bedspread. Stitch tabs in place.

Note: More tabs may be added if desired.

5. Slide tabs over curtain rod and tie back with pieces of lace.

These curtains are made much like the Matelassé curtains. Bed sheeting is used for curtains with tabs that tie around curtain rods. The simply made curtains set off a lovely, embroidered table linen that is hung under the curtains for a valance.

The table by the window is layered with a checkered piece of fabric, lace, and tea towels. Notice the attractive little lamp with a table napkin laid over the shade for accent.

FOR A LITTLE FRIEND

Remember when you were small and your mother opened her sewing box? She would remove the fabric scraps saved from all of the dresses she made. While you watched, she used the scraps to create something special just for you.

I remember rooms filled with fantasy for my stuffed bears and hand-painted porcelain dolls. She took each stitch with love and each tiny piece my mother made means as much to me today as they did when she gave them to me.

As I came to have children of my own, I carried on the same tradition, fashioning beautiful treasures and memories for my girls. I remember the look of anticipation in their eyes. Whether it was a special pillow, wall hanging, or overnight bag, they seemed to cherish it more because I made it just for them.

STORYBOOK PILLOW

*M*y grandchildren and I love the illustrations from their favorite story-books. To enjoy each one of our favorite drawings when they spend the night, I color-copy a select few onto fabric and sew them into pillows that are lovingly placed in every room of our home.

INSTRUCTIONS:

1. Determine pillow size based on sizes of art and scraps.

2. Using iron, transfer art onto muslin, following manufacturer's instructions.

3. Trim artwork, leaving ½" border all around.

4. Cut two pieces from fabric the same width as art and length as desired.

5. Cut two pieces from fabric the same length as art and width as desired.

6. Using sewing machine, stitch fabric to sides of art with rights sides together.

7. Stitch fabric to top and bottom of art and fabric with right sides together. Repeat with remaining piece.

8. Cut one piece each from batting and fabric to same dimensions as pillow front for back.

MATERIALS:

Braided cording
Fabrics: muslin; printed
Heat-transfer art
Polyester stuffing
Quilt batting: low-loft

EQUIPMENT:

Iron and ironing board
Sewing machine
Sewing needle
Straight pins
Tape measure

Illustration 1

Illustration 2

9. Place wrong side of pillow front on batting and pin in place.

10. Using needle and thread, quilt around details for dimension.

Note: Stitch as little or as much as desired.

11. Measure circumference of pillow. Cut or tear 3" x 2 times the circumference strips of fabric for ruffle.

12. Fold strip in half lengthwise and press. Using sewing machine, stitch pleats as shown in Illustration 1 on page 82.

13. Pin ruffle to pillow front as shown in Illustration 2 on page 82.

14. Stitch pillow front and back pieces with right sides together, leaving 3" opening. Trim corners and turn right side out.

15. Stuff pillow with polyester stuffing. Using needle and thread, stitch opening closed.

16. Pin cording around inside edge of ruffle and stitch in place.

PAJAMA BAG

I like to make darling pajama bags for each of my grand-daughters. They use them for a bed decoration or to carry when going to sleepover with a friend. They often, just before bedtime, button in a favorite doll or animal for sweet dreams. I have included instructions for an adorable bed jacket if you wish to make a doll shirt or jacket to match the bag.

MATERIALS:

Doll jacket or shirt
Fabrics: assorted
Quilt batting: ½"-loft
Ribbon
Sewing thread

EQUIPMENT:

Fabric scissors
Sewing machine
Sewing needle
Straight pins

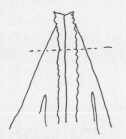

Illustration 1

INSTRUCTIONS:

1. Cut and stitch pieces of fabric to make one 15" x 24" rectangle for shell. Cut one 15" x 24" rectangle from fabric for lining. Repeat for batting.

2. Sandwich batting between shell and lining with right sides out. Using sewing needle and thread, baste together.

3. Using sewing machine, stitch rows horizontally or vertically. Optional: Using needle and thread, stitch around pattern.

4. Fold quilted piece in half widthwise with lining side out. Stitch each side closed.

5. Fold each bottom side seam of bag and stitch as shown in Illustration 1 for paper-bag corners. Turn bag right side out.

6. Tear or cut 2" x 30" strip from fabric. Pin strip around open end of bag with right sides together. Stitch in place.

7. Fold fabric over edge of bag and turn raw edge under. Stitch in place.

8. Cut four 9" lengths from ribbon for closures. Stitch two ribbons on each side of bag as shown in Illustration 2.

9. Using needle and thread stitch doll shirt or jacket for stuffed animal onto front of pajama bag.

Note: See Bed Jacket Instructions on page 86 if you wish to make a bed jacket.

Illustration 2

BED JACKET

MATERIALS:

Buttons (2)
Fabric
Quilt batting: ½"-loft
Sewing thread

EQUIPMENT:

Scissors: craft; fabric
Sewing machine
Sewing needle
Straight pins

Illustration 1

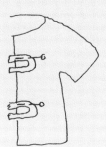

Illustration 2

INSTRUCTIONS:

1. Photocopy Jacket Pattern on page 87. Using craft scissors, cut out pattern.

2. Fold fabric in half and pin pattern with flat edge on fold for back. Using fabric scissors, cut out back. On doubled fabric (not on fold), pin and cut out pattern for jacket front. Repeat for lining and batting.

3. Sandwich batting between back and lining back with right sides out and pin layers together. Using sewing machine or sewing needle, baste edges. Repeat for left and right fronts.

4. Using sewing machine quilt in rows or using sewing needle, quilt around designs in fabric.

Note: These stitches may be very casual. Irregular stitches look primitive and whimsical.

5. Using sewing machine, stitch left and right fronts to back at shoulders with right sides together.

6. Cut two 1½" x 3" strips from fabric for button loops. Fold in thirds lengthwise and stitch as shown in Illustration 1.

7. Pin button loops to one side of jacket front at dots, adjusting loops for button size as shown in Illustration 2. Tack in place and remove pins. Trim loop ends to edge of jacket front.

8. Tear or cut 2" x 45" strips of fabric on the bias for trim on sleeves, neck, front opening, and bottom of jacket.

9. Stitch bias strip to outside sleeve edge with right sides together. Turn bias strip to inside of sleeve. Turn under raw edge and stitch in place. Trim off excess. Repeat for remaining sleeve edge, neck, front opening, and bottom of jacket. Button loops will be sewn in place during this process.

10. Stitch jacket fronts and back together at side seams with right sides together.

11. Sew buttons to opposite jacket front from loops at dots.

place on fold for back

Jacket Pattern (fits 8"–12" doll or bear)

STORYBOOK WALL HANGING

*E*veryone young at heart will be delighted with this charming doll quilt. Children and those of us who are now grown will be enchanted by the pictures and the stories each has to tell. I often hang them on my wall to replace a beautiful, but all too familiar picture, just for awhile.

MATERIALS:

Fabric
Heat-transfer art: large
  (1); small (4) (optional)
Quilt batting: ½"-loft
Ribbon
Sewing thread

EQUIPMENT:

Fabric scissors
Iron and ironing board
Sewing machine
Sewing needle

INSTRUCTIONS:

1. Using iron, transfer art to fabric. Trim to desired dimensions.

2. Cut fabric pieces for placement as shown in Illustration 1. Using sewing machine, stitch fabric pieces around large art to desired dimensions for quilt top. Optional: Small art may be used at corners.

3. Stitch ribbon around edge of art for border.

4. Place quilt top on fabric and cut out one piece for quilt back. Repeat for batting.

5. Sandwich and pin batting between quilt top and back with right sides out. Using needle and thread, baste together.

6. Using sewing machine, quilt rows of stitches. Optional: Using needle and thread, quilt around design and block as desired.

7. Stitch ribbon to edges of quilt top with right sides together. Fold ribbon to quilt back. Turn under ribbon edge and stitch in place.

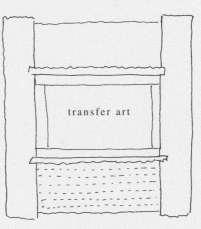

transfer art

Illustration 1

FABRIC-COVERED SCRAPBOOK

Although wedding veils and christening dresses, curtains, and tablecloths come to mind first, there are so many ways to indulge in a love of lace. From the trim on this scrapbook to the tiny snippets found on the pages inside, use your treasured lace scraps everywhere.

INSTRUCTIONS:

1. Measure width, height, and width of spine of scrapbook as shown in Illustration 1. Use the following formula to determine outside dimensions for back of cover: width + spine + 2" = back of cover width. Cut out one piece from velvet to these dimensions for width x height plus 1".

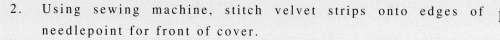

Illustration 1

2. Using sewing machine, stitch velvet strips onto edges of needlepoint for front of cover.

Note: Finished dimensions should be width plus 2" x height plus 1".

3. Cut two pieces that are ⅓ the width plus 1" x height plus 1" for inside flaps.

4. Stitch back of cover to front of cover with right sides together.

5. Fold one side flap under ½" and press. Repeat with remaining flap.

6. Pin flaps to sides of cover with right sides together. Using sewing machine, stitch together as shown in Illustration 2. Turn right side out.

Illustration 2

7. Fold top and bottom of cover in ½" as shown in Illustration 3. Press and stitch in place.

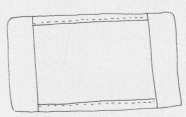

Illustration 3

MATERIALS:

Buttons: assorted
Fabrics: needlepoint or decorative; velvet
Lace doily: rectangle or square
Scrapbook
Sewing thread
Tassel with cord

EQUIPMENT:

Fabric scissors
Iron and ironing board
Sewing machine
Sewing needle
Tape measure

8. Slide book cover into ends. Pin lace to spine of book as shown in Illustration 4. Using needle and thread, tack lace in place.

9. Place buttons along edge of lace and stitch in place. Stitch one large button on front edge.

10. Tack tassel cord to back of cover and wrap tassel around large button for closure.

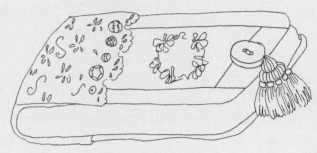

Illustration 4

Button Cards

So often, hunting for quality laces and vintage buttons involves rummaging through dusty cardboard boxes at flea markets; and I would not have it any other way. The treasures discovered hidden away are far more cherished than those that are found easily on dime-store shelves.

INSTRUCTIONS:

1. Using pencil, sketch design onto front of card.

2. Using permanent marker, draw over pencil lines. Allow ink to dry. Erase any remaining pencil lines.

3. Watercolor as desired.

4. Stitch buttons onto card.

MATERIALS:

Blank greeting card or
   card stock
Buttons: assorted
Embroidery floss

EQUIPMENT:

Embroidery needle
Eraser
Paintbrush
Pencil
Permanent marker:
   med. point
Watercolors

Button cards may be fashioned into anything. The card to the right was made using photograph transfer paper and antique buttons.

Anita/2000

gram's buttons 1925

Amy's Buttons 1910 (Blue ailies dress)

Anita/2000

HEART PILLOW

A vintage floral fabric left over from someone's cottage curtains was used to make this attractive heart pillow. It is, of course, the perfect complement to the Spring floral slipcovers on which it will lovingly be placed.

MATERIALS:

Fabric
Polyester stuffing
Sewing thread

EQUIPMENT:

Fabric marker
Pencil
Scissors: craft; fabric
Sewing machine
Sewing needle
Tracing paper

ILLUSTRATION:

1. Using pencil, trace Heart Pattern on page 96. Using craft scissors, cut out pattern.

2. Using fabric marker, trace pattern onto fabric. Using fabric scissors, cut out two hearts.

Note: Fabrics may be different for front and back.

3. Using sewing machine, stitch heart pieces with right sides together, leaving 2" opening. Clip curves. Turn heart right side out.

4. Stuff heart with polyester stuffing. Using needle and thread, stitch opening closed.

Adorable tiny hearts may be made by using a smaller heart pattern. Add a ribbon loop for hanging and embellish with lace tassels and old buttons.

cut notches after sewing

OPEN

open

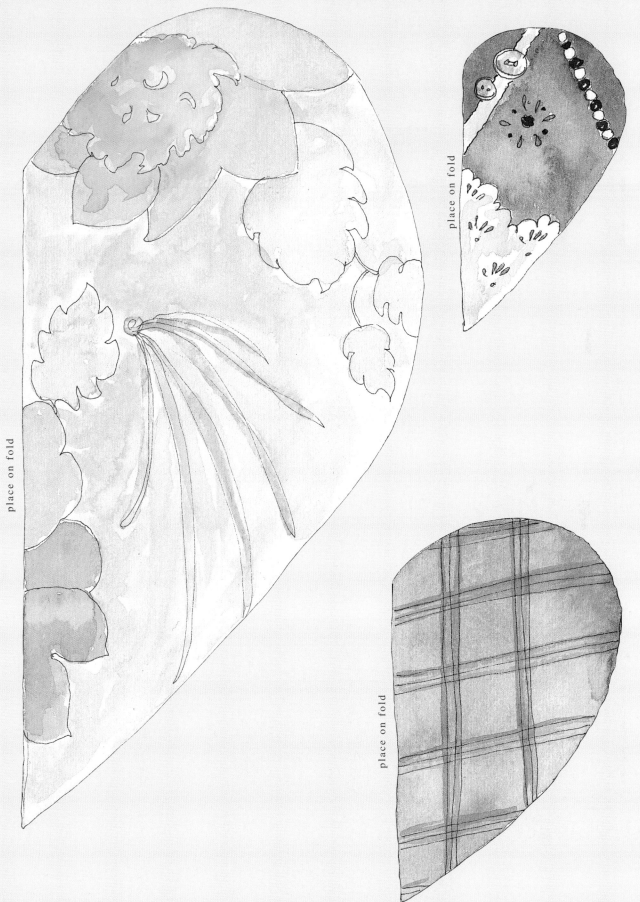

place on fold

place on fold

place on fold

CRAZY QUILT PILLOW

*C*ute, feminine, and down-to-earth, this pillow would brighten any little girl's day, while putting to use even the smallest of scraps.

MATERIALS:

Embroidery floss
Fabrics: cotton; muslin;
   velvet; wool
Lace
Polyester stuffing or
   pillow form
Velvet ribbon (optional)

EQUIPMENT:

Fabric scissors
Needles: embroidery;
   sewing
Sewing machine
Straight pins

INSTRUCTIONS:

1. Cut muslin to size for back of pillow, allowing for seam allowance.

Note: Remaining fabrics are to be used for quilted front of pillow as desired.

2. Cut block (size is your choice) for center of pillow.

3. Using sewing machine, stitch scrap pieces around center block, moving outward in design as shown in Illustration 1 until it is large enough to cover front of pillow.

4. Place muslin back on quilted front for pattern and trim off irregular edges.

5. Using embroidery needle and floss, embroider around squares with decorative stitches as shown in Illustrations 2–3.

Illustration 1

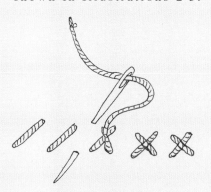

Illustration 2
Cross-stitch

Illustration 3
Straight stitch

6. Optional: Cut ribbon and lace twice the length of outside dimensions of muslin. Stitch ribbon to one edge of lace. Gather opposite edge of lace and pin to outside edge of quilted front with right sides together.

7. Place muslin and quilted front with right sides together. Using sewing machine, stitch sides together, leaving opening large enough to stuff with polyester stuffing or insert pillow form. Trim corners and turn right side out.

8. Stuff or place pillow form into cover. Using sewing needle and thread, stitch opening closed.

COME HOME TO CELEBRATE

Special occasions are particularly meaningful when we come home to celebrate them. Whether you return for a wedding ceremony, share the holidays, or commemorate your grandmother's 80th birthday, getting together with family and friends creates ties that forever bind.

Likewise, it is the little touches at home that we remember. Long after the visit is over, the sight of a sepia-toned photograph on a pillow, a lace-covered keepsake box, or the handmade decorations on the tree are that which bring back the memories of the cherished visits home.

PIN CUSHION JEWELRY BOX

*L*ace adds pristine elegance to whatever it adorns. From a Sunday dress to an antique coverlet or a jewelry box, all are more beautiful with lace.

MATERIALS:

Braid: metallic
Cardboard
Fringe
Lace fabric
Laces: assorted
Quilt batting: ⅛"-loft;
　½"-loft
Recipe box
Silk pins: #17
Trims: assorted
Victorian-style ear-
　rings (optional)

EQUIPMENT:

Craft knife
Fabric scissors
Hot-glue gun and glue
　sticks
Pencil
Stapler and staples

INSTRUCTIONS:

1. Place box lid on cardboard and trace around lid. Repeat. Using craft knife, cut out cardboard tracings.

2. Using fabric scissors and cardboard as a template, cut out six or more pieces from ½"-loft batting.

3. Stack ½"-loft batting pieces on cardboard as shown in Illustration 1.

4. Cut out one piece from ⅛"-loft batting twice the dimensions of box lid.

Illustration 1

5. Wrap ⅛"-loft batting over ½"-loft batting. Pull edges to back side of cardboard, compressing batting. Staple edges of batting in place as shown in Illustration 2.

6. Repeat Steps 4 and 5 with lace fabric.

7. Hot-glue remaining cardboard over lace and batting edges, completing pincushion.

Illustration 2

8. Hot-glue pincushion onto top of lid.

9. Hot-glue braid, fringe, lace, and trims onto edge of lid and sides of box as desired.

10. Optional: Hot-glue or attach earrings to lace around box.

11. Accent top of pincushion by pushing silk pins into batting, following lace pattern.

Tip: Small beads could be slipped on pins before inserting them into pincushion.

LACE RING PILLOW

Children's smiles light your way, their endless curiosity makes your heart sing. From one of my favorite photographs, I made this precious ring pillow for my granddaughter on her wedding day.

MATERIALS:

Fabrics: embroidered;
 muslin
Heat-transfer photo-
 graph
Laces: vintage
Polyester stuffing
Quilt batting: low-loft
Trims

EQUIPMENT:

Fabric scissors
Iron and ironing board
Sewing machine
Sewing needle
Straight pins
Tape measure

INSTRUCTIONS:

1. Determine pillow size based on size of photograph and scraps.

2. Using iron, transfer art onto muslin, following manufacturer's instructions.

3. Trim artwork, leaving ½" border all around.

4. Cut two pieces from embroidered fabric to width of art and length as desired.

5. Cut two pieces from embroidered fabric to length of art and width as desired.

6. Using sewing machine, stitch fabric to top and bottom of art with rights sides together.

7. Stitch laces and trims onto pillow top as desired.

8. Cut one piece each from batting and muslin to same dimensions as pillow front for back.

9. Place pillow front on batting and pin in place.

10. Using needle and thread, quilt around details for dimension.

Note: Stitch as little or as much as desired.

11. Pin laces around edge of pillow top.

12. Using sewing machine, stitch pillow top and back pieces with right sides together, leaving 3" opening. Trim corners.

13. Turn right side out. Stuff pillow with polyester stuffing.

14. Using needle and thread, stitch opening closed.

COME HOME TO CELEBRATE 105

QUILT GIFT STOCKING

*I*n these damaged pieces of lace, I saw something new and wonderful —
a Christmas stocking for my young granddaughter to be filled by Santa.

MATERIALS:

Beaded fabric

Braid

Fabric: linen or muslin

Heat-transfer art: 3" x 5"

Laces: assorted

Quilt batting: ½"-loft

Quilting thread

Ribbons: assorted

Sewing thread

Trims: assorted

EQUIPMENT:

Iron and ironing board

Needles: quilting;
  sewing

Sewing machine

Scissors: craft, fabric

Straight pins

Tape measure

INSTRUCTIONS:

1. Enlarge or reduce Stocking Pattern on page 108 as desired and photocopy. Using craft scissors and adding ½" all around for seam allowance, cut out pattern.

2. Pin pattern to fabric. Using fabric scissors, cut out four pieces.

3. Pin pattern onto quilt batting and cut out two pieces.

4. Using iron, transfer art onto one stocking piece, following manufacturer's instructions.

5. Place lace, ribbons, braid, trims, and beaded fabric on stocking as desired. Pin in place.

Tip: Use trims and ribbon to frame photo.

6. Using needle and thread, baste accents in place.

7. Sandwich one piece of batting between stocking front and muslin piece.

8. Using quilting needle and thread, quilt small stitches around edges of lace, ribbon, and other accents.

9. Repeat Step 7 with remaining muslin and batting pieces for stocking back.

10. Quilt back as desired.

Tip: Back may be quilted, using sewing machine.

11. Place back and front of stocking with right sides together. Using sewing machine, stitch edges of stocking with ½" seam allowance, leaving top open. Turn right side out.

12. Finish top edge by stitching ribbon or lace for cuff.

STAR TREE TOPPER

A symbol of eternity and hope, the star has long been gently tied to Christmas. Whether pieced together with scraps of fabric from Christmas' past, or made from shiny silver beads, the message it delivers remains the same.

MATERIALS:

Braid or ribbon
Buttons (assorted)
Fabrics: muslin, print
   fabric (5–6 different
   patterns)
Sewing thread

EQUIPMENT:

Fabric marker
Iron and ironing board
Polyester stuffing
Scissors: craft; fabric
Sewing machine
Sewing needle

INSTRUCTIONS:

1. Enlarge Star Pattern 182% on page 111 and photocopy. Using craft scissors, cut out pattern. Repeat for Star Center Pattern on page 111.

2. Pin Star Pattern to muslin and, using fabric scissors, cut out star for back.

3. Pin Star Center Pattern to print fabric of choice and cut out star center for front.

4. Cut or tear ½"–1" strips from print fabrics. Option: Use velvet ribbon in place of some strips.

5. Using sewing machine, stitch one fabric strip to one flat edge of star center with right sides together. Press seam open. Repeat for each side of star center, trimming off excess after pressing each seam.

Heart ornaments may be made to complement this tree topper by following Heart Pillow instructions on page 94.

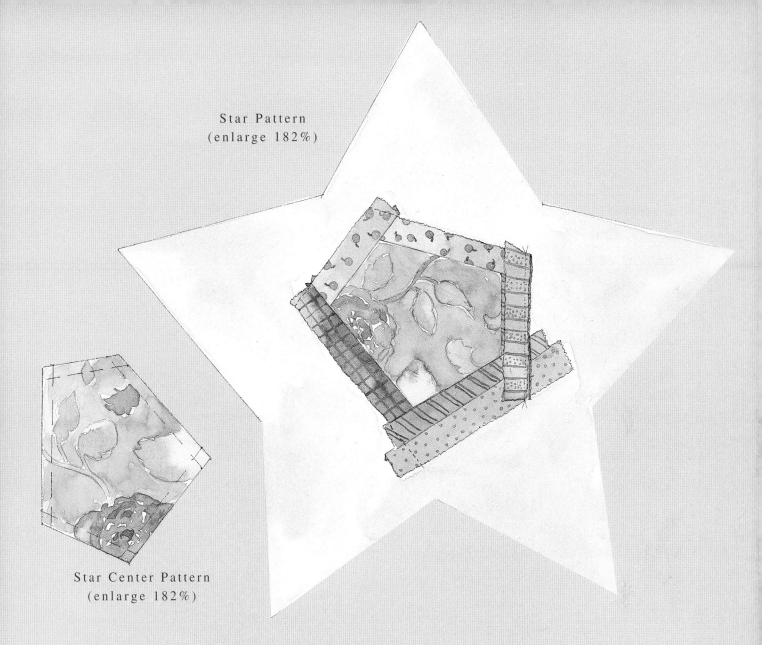

Star Pattern
(enlarge 182%)

Star Center Pattern
(enlarge 182%)

Tips: Alternate different fabrics, as desired.

Sew two strips to each side at a time. This makes the random patchwork more interesting.

6. Continue extending sides until piece is large enough to cover muslin star.

7. Place front and back pieces with right sides together. Stitch pieces together, leaving 3" opening. Carefully clip corners.

8. Turn star right side out. Stuff with polyester stuffing.

9. Using needle and thread, stitch opening closed.

10. Cut a 5" strip of ribbon or braid. Using needle and thread, stitch ends of ribbon to center back of star.

Note: Use this loop to slip over the top of your Christmas tree.

11. Optional: Stitch buttons onto star.

Keepsake Box

*T*his box of beads and broken jewelry was given to us by my husband's grandmother. The box was kept in a drawer for years and taken out on occasion to ponder the beautifully carved beads, jade, odd pearls, and a tiny, yet lovely insect pin with a wing jewel missing. Many of these very special "treasures" were used to create this beautiful box of my own. The old key and greeting card sent to me from Grandmother make this box even more special to both my husband and me.

MATERIALS:

Beads and jewelry:
  assorted
Cardboard or wooden
  stationery box
Craft glue
Decoupage medium
Greeting card
Patterned tissue paper
Ribbons: assorted
Ribbon trims: assorted

EQUIPMENT:

Hot-glue gun and glue
  sticks
Paintbrush: 1" flat

1. Decoupage tissue paper onto outside of box and lid, following manufacturer's instructions. Allow to dry.

2. Cut out card design and decoupage onto box lid. Allow to dry.

3. Using craft glue, adhere ribbons and lace onto box and lid as desired. Allow to dry.

4. Using hot-glue gun, adhere jewelry, beads, and any metallic trims onto box and lid as desired.

5. Adhere large beads onto each bottom corner of box for feet.

FABRIC-COVERED BOXES

*E*very woman loves boxes. They are places for hiding secrets, treasures, and other important "things." Plaids, checks, or toile — any fabric mix — formal or informal, are possible when you are covering boxes for such important uses. When finished, they are so beautiful when stacked together that I put them out where everyone can enjoy them.

MATERIALS:

Adhesives: decoupage
   medium or spray
   adhesive
Boxes: oval, round, or
   square
Embellishments
   (optional): beaded
   trim; beads; braid;
   buttons; lace; ribbon;
   silk flowers; tassels
Fabric, wallpaper, or
   wrapping paper

EQUIPMENT:

Hot-glue gun and glue
   sticks (optional)
Pencil
Scissors: craft or fabric
Tape measure

INSTRUCTIONS:

1. Measure diameter of lid, the lid rim, and circumference and height of box. Cut fabric, adding 1" to each measurement to allow for overlapping seams and edges.

2. Place fabric for box bottom wrong side up on work surface. Coat sides and bottom of box with spray adhesive or decoupage medium. Center and place box on fabric. Neatly bring fabric up sides of box, folding edges inside, clipping notches for turning as needed.

3. Optional: Hot-glue embellishments around circumference of lid rim.

QUILTED FABRIC ENVELOPES

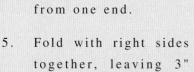

E voking visions of a formal garden in a cheerfully informal way, this quilted envelope is perfect to fill with scented sachet and neatly tuck in the folds of your fanciest lingerie.

INSTRUCTIONS:

1. Using fabric scissors, cut two 7" x 10" rectangles from fabric and one from batting.

Note: Envelopes from 4" x 7" and 5" x 9" rectangles are also shown in photo below.

2. Sandwich batting between fabrics with right sides out and pin layers together. Using sewing needle and thread, baste together.

3. Using sewing machine, quilt across width of fabric in rows the width of a zigzag foot apart.

4. Using pinking scissors, trim ½" from all sides. Round corners on one end or cut in envelope point 3" from one end.

5. Fold with right sides together, leaving 3" flap free. Stitch sides. Turn right side out.

6. Tack ribbon or braid for ties.

MATERIALS:

Fabric
Ribbon or braid
Sewing thread
Quilt batting: crib size,
   ½"-loft

EQUIPMENT:

Scissors: fabric; pinking
Sewing machine
Sewing needle

COVERED BOX WITH RIBBON TIES

A well-dressed room, even a tiny room, can make a guest feel at home. On the bedside table set this beautiful lace box. In it she can place her wedding ring, eyeglasses, and pocket book so she will know where they are in the morning.

MATERIALS:

Box with lid
Craft glue
Lace fabric
Ribbon

EQUIPMENT:

Fabric scissors

INSTRUCTIONS:

1. Cut fabric to fit box. Center box on wrong side of fabric and adhere fabric to box.

2. Repeat Step 1 for lid.

3. Cut two lengths of ribbon long enough to wrap around box and tie a bow. Adhere ribbons to top and bottom of box and lid.

4. Adhere fabric to box lid.

POUCH BAG

Beautiful treasures tucked away in shoeboxes and drawers can be brought from their hiding places and placed in delicate bags made with touches of lace. Set atop a dresser, it is a way of protecting and displaying all your keepsakes. When emptied, old memories will be sparked anew.

MATERIALS:

Buttons (2)
Embroidery floss
Fabrics (2)
Sewing thread

EQUIPMENT:

Fabric scissors
Iron and ironing board
Needles: embroidery;
  sewing
Sewing machine
Straight pins
Tape measure

INSTRUCTIONS:

1. Determine dimensions of bag, allowing ½" seam allowance all around. Cut out one piece from fabric for lining and one piece for shell.

2. Fold lining in half widthwise with right sides together. Using sewing machine, stitch sides of fabric. Repeat with shell piece. Press seams open.

3. Turn lining fabric right side out. Insert lining into shell and line up seams.

4. Stitch raw edges together, leaving 1" opening. Pull shell through opening until fabric is right side out and all seams are inside.

5. Tuck lining inside shell.

6. Using sewing needle and thread, stitch opening closed.

7. Measure circumference of pouch opening and add 8". Cut two pieces of embroidery floss to these dimensions.

8. Using embroidery needle and floss, stitch double row of stitches around bag as shown in Illustration 1 for drawstrings.

9. Thread button onto each set of drawstrings.

Optional: Tack a piece of lace fabric onto outside of shell.

Illustration 1

ENVELOPE BAG

*S*mall envelope pouches made of vintage fabric make a delicate present for yourself or a friend. They are so pretty as they hold small pieces of jewelry, a letter from your daughter, or a tiny memento from your friend Sarah's wedding.

MATERIALS:

Fabrics (2)
Sewing thread
Velcro® tabs (optional)

EQUIPMENT:

Iron and ironing board
Scissors: craft; fabric
Sewing machine
Sewing needle
Straight pins

INSTRUCTIONS:

1. Determine dimensions of bag, allowing ½" seam allowance all around. Cut out one piece from fabric for lining and one piece for shell, rounding one corner for flap as shown in Illustration 1.

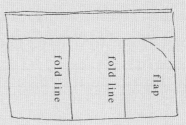

Illustration 1

2. Using sewing machine, stitch curved end of fabric pieces with right sides together as shown in Illustration 2.

3. Fold lining up to flap fold line as shown in Illustration 3 and press in place. Repeat for shell.

4. Stitch each side of lining up to flap stitching. Repeat for shell.

5. Turn flap and pockets right side out. Tuck lining into shell.

Illustration 2

6. Fold and pin raw edges in. Using sewing needle and thread, stitch opening closed as shown in Illustration 4.

7. Optional: Stitch Velcro tabs onto tab and pocket for closure.

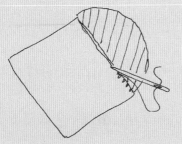

Illustration 3

Illustration 4

A book for guests to sign may be made from bits of old lace by simply following instructions on page 90.

- Pin lace to front of cover as desired, using smaller lace pieces to frame photograph.

- Stitch buttons onto cover as desired.

BUTTON FRAME

*W*hite *vintage buttons such as these once embellished lacy summer after-noon dresses. What stories they could tell — long forgotten days in the country, birthday parties, and church on Sunday. Gathered together around this delicate frame they are still part of what I hold most dear.*

MATERIALS:

Buttons: assorted, small;
  specialty (4)
Craft glue
Double picture mat

EQUIPMENT:

Hot-glue gun and glue
  sticks
Tweezers

INSTRUCTIONS:

1. Apply craft glue on
    mat 2" at a time.
    Using tweezers and
    beginning at edges, place small buttons on glue. Continue
    until frame is covered. Allow to dry.

2. Using hot-glue gun, adhere one specialty button to each cor-
    ner of frame.

BUTTON BOX

In a sitting room where late afternoon light filters through the lace curtains, I love to surround myself with pristine images of white. For me, they add a slight touch of sentiment to my afternoon. On the table next to my chair where I sip hot tea, is my Aunt Sara's clock and a small button box I made with buttons from my mother's button tin.

MATERIALS:

Buttons: specialty;
  white, assorted
Craft glue
Lace: 1"-wide
Wooden heart-shaped
  box (with hinged lid)

EQUIPMENT:

Hot-glue gun and glue
  sticks
Tweezers

INSTRUCTIONS:

1. Apply craft glue on top of box lid 2" at a time. Using tweezers and beginning at edges, place white buttons on glue. Allow to dry.

Note: Make certain to leave hinge area free of glue.

2. Using craft glue, adhere lace to sides of box and lid.

3. Using hot-glue gun, adhere specialty buttons to center of lid.

4. Using hot-glue gun, adhere additional buttons onto lace as desired.

Fill an attractive bottle such as an old cheese shaker with buttons. Adhere scraps of lace and buttons onto the lid. How could an avid button collector resist this charming way to display their collection?

Metric Conversion Table

cm—Centimetres
Inches to Centimetres

inches	cm	inches	cm	inches	cm	inches	cm
⅛	0.3	5	12.7	21	53.3		
¼	0.6	6	15.2	22	55.9	38	96.5
½	1.3	7	17.8	23	58.4	39	99.1
⅝	1.6	8	20.3	24	61.0	40	101.6
¾	1.9	9	22.9	25	63.5	41	104.1
⅞	2.2	10	25.4	26	66.0	42	106.7
1	2.5	11	27.9	27	68.6	43	109.2
1 ¼	3.2	12	30.5	28	71.1	44	111.8
1 ½	3.8	13	33.0	29	73.7	45	114.3
1 ¾	4.4	14	35.6	30	76.2	46	116.8
2	5.1	15	38.1	31	78.7	47	119.4
2 ½	6.4	16	40.6	33	83.8	48	121.9
3	7.6	17	43.2	34	86.4	49	124.5
3 ½	8.9	18	45.7	35	88.9	50	127.0
4	10.2	19	48.3	36	91.4		
4 ½	11.4	20	50.8	37	94.0		

Index